Lovely

A porcelain doll
Sitting on the shelf
A ribbon made of red satin silk
Curly brown locks
Big blue eyes
A twinkle of mischief hidden
Flowers and lace
Tea by the lake
A smile shared secretly
Diamonds on rings
Pearls on strings
Stockings and Janes
A little girl with such fame
Do you think she's lovely?

Little Lucy Lilica

Little Lucy Lilica was loved by everyone
Never never never by a person was she shunned
Perfect perfect that she was
Big brown eyes
Blonde hair undone
A twinkle, twirl
Look she is there
Lovely lovely she was called
Gentle gentle as a dove
Pure pure pure pure
But she was all alone
No one no one none at all
Could see why she took the fall
They couldn't see her cry at night
Or want her mommy there for light
Mommy was gone
Daddy was gone
Even Good Old Bruno
A little Cinderella in a fairy tail gone wrong
No evil step mother to lock her up
No prince to come and save her
There was only her in this special Wonderland
Little Lucy Lilica hated everyone
Stone cold heart
And razor tongue
She fooled them
She fooled them
She fooled them you see
They took her Papa away from her
They shot her mother dead
Even Good Old Bruno's head was put over the fence
Stupid stupid that they were
Evil evil to the core
Blind blind nothing more
Little Lucy Lilica was plotting what to do
Even if they all loved her they would never have a clue
She jumped in delight
As her plan took flight
Little Lucy Lilica burned to death last night

Ugly

I wanna be like your girlfriend
She's pretty, pure, sweet, and strong
She's a beautiful person
I can clearly see why you chose her over me
Why you don't love me
Her eyes are like the forest of fairies
Her lashes so pretty
Her lips always hold a smile
Her hair is shiny, glossy, and silky
She's tall but short enough for you to rest your head on hers
Her voice is light and angelic
Her mind free of the worries of the world
You wish to keep her mind that way
She never wanted to resort to violence and is scared of gruesome scenes
She's perfect in every way
I'm so ugly
Both inside and out
I'm sarcastic, cruel, cold, and barely caring
The windows to my soul are so big anyone could see through them
My eyelashes just give them a scary effect
My lips are too big and pouty
My hair is thick and easy to frizz and tangle so it's barely let down
My voice is low and unnoticeably broken but positively negative and bland
My mind is filled with the error of our ways
You made me realize them
I wouldn't mind throwing a punch and can come up with the most gruesome scenes possible
I am flawed and unfixable
You don't love me because I'm ugly
I know I'm ugly
I have fits
I hurt and am hurt
I break and am broken
I cry when I think no one can see me
Just so I don't break my unfeeling image you all have of me
Just so you won't call me ugly even more
Though you never say it directly
I hear what you say to them
But I can still love you
Because the way you treat me when its just us gives me hope that you keep extinguishing and rekindling
Sometimes...
Sometimes I wanna break through my image
Sometimes I wanna be like you,

So kind, strong willed, good humored, and beautiful
Sometimes I wanna be like her,
Innocent, loving, helpful, and beautiful
Sometimes I wanna be pretty too
I wanna hear you say "You look pretty right now"
Even if it's just once
So I can hold onto it forever
Just don't lie to me when you say I'm pretty
Because we all know I'm not
Because she's here
Because I'm not her
Because I'm just ugly

Under Your Skin

When I first saw what was under your skin
Beneath your mask
I was horrified and scared
You were truly a demon in the body of an angel
Same with your girlfriend
You were both vicious and unforgiving
Bloodthirsty and sadistic
Cruel and deadly
Ugly
But I was able to hold you down
Because I was more than you
I was the wielder of a stone heart and grudges
Murderous and sadistic
Cruel, cold, stubborn, and maniacal
Uglier
But under my mask
When I shed my skin
I care and worry
I coddle and are possessive
I'm shy and insecure
To sum it up I'm messed up and shattered
But what was under your skin made me feel better
Made your punishment not as bad
But still worse
Because what was under your skin
Was me

Voices

They voices in my head
Never seem to stop
They're haunting me
Taunting me!
Forcing me to listen to my wrongs
They sound like Maya and Brittany and Shane and Mark!
Like everyone in this room
They're killing me slowly
I can feel their icy fingers
Gripping my neck
Clawing my throat
Smothering the life changing breath from me
Their evil eyes filled with hunger for my pain
Captivating me with their amber glow
Go away!
Go away!
I want you to not be seen
Not to be heard by me
Their words are like silken daggers
So smooth and rich
Yet piercing me each and every time
The voices keep telling me I'm a terrible person
That...
That...
That I deserve to die

Running Away

If I could,
You should know,
I'd run right out the door
Not daring to look back at all your confused faces,
And the teacher running after me
No one should dare to stop me
Running off campus
Just to escape
The demons staring
With their hungry eyes
Don't chase after me
Or else the demons will devour you
Don't follow
Or else your fate will be sealed
Running down the highway,
I don't dare to stop
Or else they will catch me
They called my parents
And now they're looking for me
But it's too late,
I don't know where I went
But I sit here,
In the middle of this clearing,
Wondering what I'll do now
My thoughts were only on running away

Reaching Out

Alone in the darkness
Nothing around
Solitude and Blindness
Not even a sound

Nothing to hold me
No light at the end of the tunnel
Nothing I can see
Not knowing where the sun fell

Not knowing where it would rise
Shrouded by guilt so strong
Drowning in truths that are now lies
Kicked out of where I belong

I know not where I am
Wondering but uncaring
Unlike the frightened lamb
My sanity is now tearing

In here it is so cold
They betrayed the trust meant for them
To the devil my soul they sold
Like a flower plucked by the stem

Living breathing screaming dreaming
To finally be released
My revenge is full proof what's felt like years I've been scheming
But I'm being stalked by my inner beast

This revenge is not worth it
Not what I desire
I still have my wit
I just do not want them to put out my fire

What I long for is someone
Someone for me
Please, anyone
Who won't let me be

Save me from the shadows
Save me from myself
Wishing to see the weeping willows
Can you see me in yourself?

Broken and lonely
For one last time
Finally I've decided
I reach out my hand
Into the foreboding blackness
Waiting for something
Anything at all
I keep my hand outstretched
Then a flash of light
When I open my eyes
Your hand is grasping mines tight

Grabbing Her Hand

I watched her day by day
As she blindly struggled with her life
Then she began losing her way
Her friends gave her unimaginable strife

The roses they sent were beautiful
But I saw her cut her hands
The thorns are what she got for being dutiful
And obeying their every commands

I could tell she was lonely
She knew what was going on
Wondering if only
She knew they were artists of con

Never once looking my way
Always staring at her
Constantly walking away
People rushing by in a blur

Forgotten and unseen
Is what is you and me
Against this glass wall we lean
Waiting to be shattered by she

There was so much she just didn't know
Unbelieved and unheard
So much I could show
Crazy and absurd

Who could tell us what life is?
Who could tell us what is love?
Certainly not hers or his
Certainly not a dove

She's plotting revenge
But realizes her error
There was nothing to avenge
She was no longer full of terror

Everyone surrounded
Like a committee of vultures
Hateful and astounded
Strings of insults of different cultures

As she glanced at me
I saw she was pleading
Pushing though the crowd
Her eyes were closed
Ignoring the confused and irked looks
I made it to her with her hand on the floor
I grabbed hers with both of mine
And squeezed it tight
Finally she opened her eyes
And she saw me
Finally she smiled
Finally she could see

Where Did You Go?

I miss the times we spent together and the laughs that always followed us
When you were around 24/7 and I had a panic attack when I didn't know where you were
Can you come back to me please?
I miss you so much
All we would do is play tag and talk
Have you outgrown me?
You've moved on, and I'm stuck in one endless motion of childishness
You have new friends now
Have you forgotten me?
I miss you too much
I cry when no one can hear me
I want my best friend back!!!
Why did we drift so far apart?
Did I do something wrong
Tell me why you left
Do you even see me?
Can you see past my smiles and find that longing hidden so deep within my eyes?
Countless times I wanted to call your name just to get your attention
Even if only for a little bit
I want to include your name
But what would you think?
I want to talk to you again
Just one last time
So I can ask
"Best buddy, where did our friendship go?"

Red Thread of Fate

Little Boy
Little Boy
Quick Run Away

Little Girl
Little Girl
Don't Take The Path Gone Astray

Children Children of the Light
Don't Be Swayed by Darkness Bright
Don't Be Foolish and Lose Your Sight
The Star Will Surely Bring You Fright

A Child A Child
Long Ago
A Child A Child
So Pretty So

That Child That Child
They Went the Wrong Way
That Child That Child
Faced the Demon Called Fate

Fate Was Sleeping
Sleeping Sound
In Fate's Hand Red Ribbons Bound

The Child The Child
A Mischievous Child
Took the Ribbons Fate Had Bound
And Slowly Slowly
One By One
Unraveled the Ribbons It was Done

A Thread So Red
Thread So Simple
Woke the Beast
And Caused A Ripple

The Child The Child
The Child Is Gone
Fate Had Showed The Child
What the Child Had Caused
The Child Immediately Took The Knife To Heart

The Child The Child had broken many ties
The Child The Child forced truths to become lies
So Fate decided to never show again
In the star so bright Fate is spinning more threads

So follow not the star of night
For like The Child you will lose your sight
And Fate, oh Fate, will make you see
The lives of many ruined by thee

Remember Me

Remember the boy in your dreams
Remember the girl in your thoughts
Remember the times we spent together
So the memories will never part
Soon we will be separated
Gone from each others lives
We may never meet again
after we depart
To leave
To start anew
It's difficult to do
If life were easier than this
We wouldn't rue
Chances missed
Opportunities taken
Friendships broken
and lost on the wind
The red ribbons and threads
That bound us together
Have unwoven and been ripped apart
All we need to do is take the first step
The step that seals our fate
No more going back
No more wishing on that star
Our paths are straying away
Our ties are being severed
What I'm asking of you
Is impossible I know
But if you could possibly
After it's all official and done
After we've moved on with our lives
After time has passed
If I promise to remember you,
Could you possibly remember me too?

Transparency

Every day you do not see me
Every day my fear grows more
Every time someone looks my way
I fill with hope
Only for it to deflate again
Each time you walk through me
I feel the pain
The pain of loneliness
The pain of seclusion
The pain of being unloved
The pain of being unknown
No one has ever seen me
I'm just empty transparency

Eyes

You call me beautiful
Through me you see
But the world I see
is upside down
and beautiful physically
The images I see
Images I've seen
You refuse to remember
Because of me
If he says you have beautiful eyes
He talks about me
Never you
If she's lost in your eyes
She gazing at me
Not you
I wish I weren't me
Everything is so physical
Physical only
I wish to truly see
Not what is forced upon me
I'm searching
But my range is limited by you
If only you knew what you took for granted
Thoughts and feelings
What about me?
You take me for granted
Just wait until I refuse to start

If Only

If only humans were like the snow
So pretty and pure, soft and fragile
Different like each and every individual snowflake
Yet so cold, so colorless
The dirtiness can clearly be seen

If only life was like the sky
So full of vividness, so vast, so full of fluffy clouds for when we fall
Anything would be possible
Yet can become so dangerous and hateful with the storm
Rage so easily seen

If only peace was like music
Constantly flowing everywhere with it's beautiful melodies
A different song for everything good
Yet can cause conflict
Music is so easy to mute

If only love were not like a flower
A bud waiting for the right person
Blooming so beautifully
Yet dies so soon
Only for this painful process to be repeated again

Our world is full of people who murder without thinking of the individual lives lost, upset because they lost their peace due to their own selfishness do not try to love again

But

Our world is also full of people who try to appreciate each and every life because they know peace cannot be achieved with hatred and rage, but acceptance and love

Wind Chime

There it hangs, out on the porch
Juggling with each breeze
A soft sound warm like a torch
The wind gives a slight sneeze

There the wind chime let's out it's sound
A gentle tingle all about
Brining peace to all on the ground
Sweeping away unpleasantness and doubt

Yet so sad as well as fragile
That poor little trinket
The wind carries so very agile
That to the wind chime, it does not think it

It bears all the sorrows
And tries to give joy
It can wait for the morrow
To the people it is just a toy

The wind makes it listen to all the pain from below
The wind chime is really a melancholy thing
Swirling around it so dreadfully slow
Yet still its soft voice longs to sing

So sing little wind chime
Let out your song
You need not bear all the sorrows alone
It's okay for you to make yourself feel better
Think of all the people whose days you've made shine

The Little Things

We're no longer together
We're no longer one
I've come to accept it
Because it's something so big
But it still hurts
Yes I admit
If you bother to glance, even at all
When our eyes meet
Your eyes are so dull
I no longer see
The love from long ago
I remember when our fingers
Brushed together so slightly
The secret smiles we shared
Our words with double meanings
Our gazes full of love
True you may think it's stupid
That I held on to that ring
I can't bring myself to take it off
Because of the memories it holds
The arguments we had
You think those little things are stupid
But those little things make up
The biggest things of all
I miss your smile
I miss your gaze
I miss our fights
I miss everything we had
Yes I hold on to the little things
Because they once brought me joy
And you still don't seem to understand
It's the little things
That hurt most of all

Who Knows?

As I sit here, I can't help but smile
Even though this is a time of mourning
People stare as if I'd gone crazy
Maybe I should have never confessed
You were a dear friend
Maybe if I had kept my mouth shut this could have been avoided
You wouldn't have left
Maybe, just maybe
Who's to say what would have happened?
They all look at me with pitiful gazes
I don't need that
What I need to do is thank you
Why is what you would ask
Well thank you
Thank you for always being there for me
Thank you for making me happy even if only for a little while
Thank you for those sweet smiles you gave me each day
Thank you for loving me

As a friend...

How I wish you could have accepted my feelings
Maybe things wouldn't be as hard as now
But still,
Thank you for everything you've done
I'll continue to love you
Even through this painful period
Things will get better eventually
I promise I'll never forget you
And pray you never forget me

Past Chances

Staring in the mirror while hating me
I'm staring at your lies while hating you
Now closing my eyes I don't want to see
Screaming at the sky, an angry wind blew
Why did this happen? Why did I let it?
My soul is encased in evil solitude
Waiting for this ice heart to be relit
But it's time for my story to conclude
Spiders of love creep down these shaken bones
Trying to open my eyes that seal shut
Crushed one by one because of fearful woes
Corpses in shells easily burned like chestnuts
Never again will I reanimate
Now, never again will chances I waste

Solitude

I sit here by this open window
Raindrops gliding down the glass
This house is so big
So empty
So full of sweet memories
Memories of you and me
Looking at the garden bombarded by rain
I see little bluebells crying in pain
The only flowers you wanted me to plant
Now I can see why
I always wondered why you picked them
But I can see your intentions
They symbolize solitude
You planned to leave me alone from the start
Right after you got her where you wanted her
How could I have been so easily deceived?
My head is pounding
My vision blurring
My stomach churning
You threw me away
I never mattered to you
But after tonight
When everything is complete
It will be you looking out this window
Staring at those pitiful bluebells
With this emptying, killing feeling of solitude
I swear it

I Can't Love You Anymore

Unrequited love is a disgusting thing
Everlasting love flies on plastic wings
Love at first sight is physical only
It is impossible for this heart to love wholly
This racing heartbeat
This cat-tied tongue
The secret glances
They just can't go on
Fumbling mind
Flushing face
Rising temperature
My being is changing at an unsteady pace
I feel me changing
I know I am
These confusing symptoms
This hated love
Never will I confess
Never will those three forbidden words leave my lips
Never again will these symptoms arise
Cause these feelings will need to disappear
You're a drug and I can't seem to get enough
Soon I'll be at the point of no return
Then we'll see who gives in first
You never seem to leave my mind
Constantly intruding when you have the time
Infiltrating my heart while my guard is down
Stealing my sanity
Eating my ways
All this while licking the plate
But my resolve is unwavering
Oh never again
I can't stand to see your eyes or face
You disgust me
You scare me
You intrigue me for sure
But honestly honey, I'm sorry,
I can't love you anymore

Shattered Dreams and Cracked Hearts

One day I had hope
The next day it was gone
The same day I found love
But then it was con
The one that I loved
Had shattered my dreams
Dreams made of glass
That he broke easily
The shards of hope I once stored
Found their way to my heart
And there they slowly
Tore me apart
The man had already
Walked out my door
Now merely a memory
Nothing more
A memory filled with anger and pain
A memory that
Will never go away
The dreams I once had
Still lay broken on the floor
I couldn't pick up
The pieces anymore
There had been thousands laying there
But now only a few hundred
Long ago I thought
I could pick them back up
And the dreams would come back to me
But it's been years since that thought
And they still lay in front of me
This heart of mine
Has healed but with scars
The crack down the middle
Grows bigger each year
The crack will eventually
Reopen my heart
But until then
My life can't depart

Dreamer

She was a dreamer
Slave to her imagination
An ignorant fool
With hopes for the future
A future that wouldn't come true
She wanted to be a princess
An officer
A wife and mother as well
She wanted true love
She wanted a happily ever after
She wished and wished
On the north star
She wished and wished
11:11 was never far
Shooting stars gave her strength
As did four leaf clovers
She believed if she kept wishing
And gathering good luck
All her dreams would come true
No one had the heart
To tell her she was wrong
She did nothing much
She rode the ride
But didn't pay
She reached mountain but never climbed
Now how does she feel
Simply crying
For this thing called
Reality?

Transition Climb

To see you again is so bittersweet
Our feelings have vanished, gone on the wind
You long disappeared when the hailstorms weep
Leaving my mind and heart is your great sin
Knowing the truth and accepting it too
Running away and begging me to stay
The old me stares and then begins to rue
She was lost and then she was lead astray
The new me would laugh at her foolishness
As she would continue to climb the mount
Grinning at the monster called happiness
She hit the wolf in the face, on the snout
She spat in the face of love and hid well
Let's hope you can live, and about her tell

A Dream Long Lost

In this world today
I screamed and screamed
In the world yesterday
I dreamed and dreamed
A promise kept forever only
A promise false forever only
I'm crying crying in this place
My heart is dying dying in its space
I wished for a place
Where I could be free
A place where we
Could smile happily
I never would have thought
I never would have cried
I never would have loved
If only you had died!
A smile so evil yet so false
A gaze so burning yet scorching
A love frozen over
A love long lost
A dream frozen over
A dream long lost

Love's Today, Love's Yesterday

Yesterday love was with you
In the morning at 8 we were shy
Barely glancing at each other
By 9 we were still apart
10 we said hi but that was it
Nobody knew a thing
11 we talked shortly
Just chit chat cause our friends weren't there
12 PM, Noon we became friends
It was amazing how fast it came about
1 PM we were getting closer
With little inside jokes and gestures
2PM You asked the question
And I had said yes
3PM everyone knew
And we didn't care
It was that short moment of bliss
We both shared
4PM we went on a date
But that wasn't the end of it
So many followed after
5PM we kissed
It was short and sweet
You promised that
You would never leave me
6PM we were closest
Our friends all laughed
I had hoped it would never end
7PM we started drifting
Further and further apart
It confused me so much
8PM it was heartbreaking
As I just sat crying
You had come up to me
Stoic and unfeeling
What you said tore me to pieces
"I don't love you anymore"
I spent the rest of the night
Getting over you

Today this morning by 8 the new boy came
I looked at him in suspicion
And prejudice from before
9AM he was staring

Staring at me
My friends laughed
At the red in his face
10AM he was trying
To talk to me
I ignored him coldly
As he blabbered on and on
It's 11 now, and he's still here
Talking about stupid things
Is this what love does?
Makes you stone?
He suddenly looked me strange
By noon I knew
Why he looked so strange
He heard my question
About love
And now he pities me
I don't need his sympathy
1PM he wasn't there
To tell me stories of camping and guns
He stayed far away
He wouldn't look at me
And suddenly I felt alone
2PM was lonely
Without him there
He was talking to her
And the jealousy bubbled inside
3PM I greeted first
He acted all cool
But I could tell he was excited
Was that all he wanted?
A response?
4PM I responded slightly
As he talked rapidly
I let out a small smile
I was becoming me
5PM he seemed nervous
I already knew why
I just hoped
He wouldn't cry
But when he asked
I surprised myself
6PM it wasn't that bad
He made me laugh again
And was slowly healing me
7PM we were only talking on the phone

He said we would talk it slow
He truly was amazing
I just didn't deserve him
8PM I was happy
Because I no longer needed that other man
Love is strange
But love is wise
The man with me now
Just won't let me cry
I spent the rest of the night wishing
He would be there for Love's Tomorrow Morning

Clockwork Hearts

Beating beating
Now no more
Spinning spinning
Now it's stopping
The springs have stopped pumping blood
The gears are stuck in place
Cogs are missing needed wanted
Feelings are missing needed wanted
I can't hear
That tedious tick
I can't hear
That malicious tock
I can't feel
The hands spinning and spinning
The gears can no longer shift
The clock is broken
The clock has stopped
I'm dead weight
Without the tick
Without the tock
I'm dead weight
No more tricks
No more locks
The little birdie can no longer talk
My heart is malfunctioning, stopping, broken
The clock has malfunctioned, stopped, broke
Can you wind back up my heart?

Spiderweb Thoughts

This intricate design
That's called my mind
A place where ideas are woven and born
Sliding around and sticking to place
Get stuck and never get out
Rarely forgotten
But sometimes forever lost
Crawling around
Hunting their prey
The predators that lock away my thoughts
Eaten
Poisoned
Killed
A maze with death at every turn
This spider mind
With it's spiderweb thoughts

Schizophrenia and Drugs

Alone in your room
Watching them tormenting you
These new friends that follow you everywhere
They came from nowhere
Telling you to never say a word
Exchange your life for their fun
They'll kill you if you don't
Letting them do as they please
Not knowing where they came from
Not knowing why they came now
You find out one day
When your sister walks into the room
She doesn't see them
She walks right past
She gets her homework
And through them again
That's when you realize you have -------------

After that realization you began to change
And their attacks felt so real
You didn't know what was reality or hallucination anymore
To set your mind straight
You made a mistake
And then your being was permanently changed
Reading the same book as if there was something to gain
What happened to the person who was always on time?
Just So hard working and so very kind
Never skipped classes and got all A's
Well apparently, you'll never be the same
After going to those foolish kids behind school
You never really thought they were that cool
But after they gave you ----- your opinion changed
And now it's your life you waste

Heroin became your heroine
And cocaine your favorite scent
You're stupid decision will end it all
Because when it fades away the torment will commence
And that torment will be worse than before
After each and each dose you take
Never occurring in your mind that someone could help you
Now when you think there's no more escape
How can we help you if you can't awake?

Psych Ward

Seeing all those poor kids
Who seemed to have gone crazy
Hallucination violation and the want and urge to hurt or kill
The secret feeling of uncertainty as imaginary friends pretend to thrill
Pharmacies in their bodies
Spirits in their heads
The hint of fear of causing hurt
The knowing that they will
The knowing that their families fear them
The fear of themselves
Thinking that maybe they can be normal
Then the demons come again
Tempting them to strangle and steal
Take a chainsaw to your mother's neck
Is what they whisper so sweetly
Jump off the third story
Is what they shriek with glee
Sent here because they unknowingly went insane
Wondering if anyone can save them from their dementia
Angry at everything
With no one to blame
All alone in their room
Leaving them to their evil's will
Missing their families
But knowing the risks
Stuck here in the Psych Ward
Not really planning to leave

7 Minutes Dead

Fields of Black
Skies of Red
Flowers of Fire
People of Dead

Day One I was walking
Not knowing where to go
Constantly following
The demon in front
She never seemed to mind me
I guess that was good
I was lost in a world
Where you're alone no matter what
No one needs you
You don't need anyone
But I needed someone
And no one was there

Day Two she continued
Ignoring me
As I followed her to work
In this strange fantasy
The world was burning
The pressure was high
Even while suffering
I could not cry
Her job was strange
We were on the surface
We approached a car crash
She lifted her scythe
And brought it down
Through the poor child's face
No matter how gruesome
No matter how disturbing
No matter how sorrowful
I couldn't look away

Day Three it was routine
She never talked to me
The sinners all stared
As if mocking me
They giggled and sneered
And threw rocks at my head
When a rock came at her

I pushed her out of the way
And so she avoided
A stone to the face
She looked at me cruelly
Just like the other two days
But I continued smiling
Despite all the pain

Day Four she looked at me
Much differently than before
She seemed less sinister
And more so afraid
She was agitated and cautious
Always on edge
So to ease her suffering
I grabbed her hand
And my smile wouldn't stray away
My pain I could ignore
Because her ice cold hand
And it's unpleasant contrast to the flames
Was all I needed
And she didn't bother to push me away

Day Five was the best of all
In this world of hell
Even when pushed around
Even when burned by the air I breathe
When feeling the affects of poisoned food and yet not dying
When there was no music and dancing
When I'm alone but me
I found someone who might need me
The demon named Nephthys
Who finally spoke to me

Day Six started confusing
And ended in pain
I looked around for Nephthys
In this blood-stained place
The demons all jeered
And said my efforts were useless
But I continued to search
Despite my growing fatigue
The oceans were bloody
But she was not swimming
The sky was so frightening
But she was not flying

The world was on fire
And no matter how much I screamed,
in senseless agony
Nephthys wouldn't come to me
It was then when I understood
Nephthys was gone
And finally
I cried

Day Seven I finally
Felt dead and numb
I had no one to follow
No hand to hold
No death to watch
No place to call home
True I never had a home here
But she was the best I had
Thinking about how I got there
I couldn't remember a thing
The imps continued
To poke pitchforks at me
I ignored them coldly
Before a voice spoke to me
"You're too much of a nuisance to her,
It hinders the death."
The voice was raspy and revolting
So high pitched like nails on a chalkboard
So low like hollow tunnel
Then I was whisked away

When I opened my eyes
Laying in the hospital bed
Blurs of faces around me
The heart monitors steady beep
I saw Nephthys in the corner
Staring at me
Invisible to everyone
Then she faded away
That's when I realized
I'd been Seven Minutes Dead

The Girl Who Won Death

A long long time ago
A wrong wrong little girl was born
A song
A song
A song
A song
A song for her was sung

She cried and cried
While her mother died and died
Her father sighed and sighed and sighed and sighed
A shot
A shot
A shot
was fired
a Shot
a Shot
a Shot
Was Fired

The clock is ticking ticking ticking **tocking**
The little girl was wishing wishing *missing* **locking**
Tick Tick goes her heart of clock
Tock Tock, will her heart talk?
Why Why goes her brain
Questions left unanswered

PAPA PAPA oh he was gone
PAPA PAPA he took the fall
Mama Mama oh she was gone
Mama Mama she stopped the song
The Reaper the Reaper the Reaper has come
Oh Reaper Reaper the game has begun

Smiling smiling oh she was SMILING
Dying dying oh she was DYING
Screaming screaming oh she was screaming
Screaming in rage at the being called Death

Cloaked in black
Cloaked in black
Stained in red

Stained in red

A little girl facing a being called Death
A being A being A being she Saw
Bleeding bleeding bleeding she waS

With her blood was forged a sword
With her blood a sword was forged
Against Death she Slashed and Slashed
Against Death she hacked and hacked

Finally oh finally Death had disappeared
Finally oh Finally she had fought her fears

A long long time ago
A wrong wrong little girl was born
This wrong wrong little girl was special
This wrong wrong little girl won the devil.

Why?

Unescapable Fate
Inevitable Death

Choices Made
Decisions Changed
Minds Played

Life Taken
Life Shaken
Life Given
Life Waken

Hearts Broken
Love Lost
Threads Unbound

Dead Wishes
Red Hopes
Golden Fears
Stolen Tears

Darkness Raging
Shadows Flaming
Light Calming
Brightness Fading

Why her?
Why me?
Why you?
Why he?

And if
And if
And if

Secrets Told
Shyness Bold
Slyness Seen
Extremely Keen

If I
If you
If we
Could we?

Should we?
Would we?
But why?

Questions Unanswered
Desires Unheard
Dreams Grounded
Angels Fallen

My Angel

Ever since I was a little girl
An angel watched over me
He was fair
He was lovely
He was meant for me
He loved me
He hugged me
I loved and hugged him back
He protected me
He whispered so softly
For that was his voice
A long time ago
Someone stole his voice
But not long ago
I stole his heart
He was meant for me
Not another
I took the knife up
And my angel went under

Fallen Angel

Fallen Angel laughing there
This is what They mean
Life is never legitimate

Fallen Angel with You,
Nothing is sincere
Fighting it won't help any longer

You cried and cried
But no one heard
They were too wrapped up in their exuberant shouts

Fallen Angel, face the truth
No one can see You
No one ever has

What made You think they would now?
Fallen Angel, it's time to say
Goodbye

Parent Fight

I watch them fight
Like every other day
Those parents of mine

They yell and curse
Making me upset
But that they will never know

Mommy, stop doing this
You always end up angrier
I want this all to stop

Daddy, that's enough
Stop being so stubborn
Things need to change

If I died tomorrow
Would anyone notice?
Would anyone shed a tear?

Of course they would
But would never know
How many tears I'VE shed

I feel like a broken bird
I can't fly back home
I can't do a thing

Why did you start fighting?
Can we go back to when we were happy?
Is it because I grew up?

Mommy picked up her bags and stormed out the door
She got in her car and drove away
I ran after her, as fast as I could
But she was already gone

Daddy went back into the house
And turned on the TV as if nothing happened
I stand in the soaking cold rain, tears mixing with it
My breath is caught in my throat, but I can still whisper
"Mommy, don't go... It's my birthday..."

Abuse

Ever since
Mama left
Papa was never the same

Each week was a new woman
But they all seemed the same
Papa knew that I thought this

He seemed to understand
But it all started when he hit me
And it has never stopped since

Why did Mama
Have to go
And leave me all alone?

Every night
I cry and cry
Papa seems to enjoy it

Maybe he wants me to suffer
Because he is too
Maybe he wants me to realize

He started taunting me
Putting me down
Making me feel like trash

Ever since
Mama left
Papa's been abusing me

Drugs

Josie said
She found something
That could ease our pain

Both our lives
Had been ruined
When our Mommies went away

She said to me
"You should try some!"
But I already knew what it was

Josie found some drugs
Meth to be exact
She started using it

Even sneaking some into class
She tried to get me to try some
She said she'd keep bugging me until I do

Finally,
Some months later
I became addicted too

Mommy's Death

One day
When I came home from school
Daddy said someone was there to see me

I went to my room
And there she was
Mommy was standing there

In her hand were my drugs
She said nothing
And just stared

I didn't know what to say
She stared
With shock and despair

She walked out the door
And try as I might
She wouldn't face me

The next day
On the news
Mommy died last night

Suicide

Tonight's the night
I finally do it
The night I take my life

I don't blame Josie
Even if she gave me the drugs
That made Mommy go away

I don't blame Daddy
For abusing me
And letting this all happen

I don't blame Mommy
For walking out the door
And setting the tracks for a crash

I blame myself
For allowing me to be tempted
For letting her walk away

So Mommy,
In apology
I'll do something special

A silver shine
In the faint,
Dark moonlight

I ended it all
With one fell swoop
Don't worry Papa

I'm with Mama tonight

Sweet Intoxication

I can't have you
I can't want you
I shouldn't have you
I shouldn't want you
I made a mistake
Now I can't break away
I cut off my wings
And on my head a horn grew
You're constantly seeping into my brain
Closing my throat
Paining my lungs
My heart is on fire
This love is forbidden
I opened Pandora's box
And now I'm paying the price
But I can't get enough
Your scent
Your touch
The look in your eyes
Drives me insane
You know I want you
You know I wish for you
And you taunt me
Spreading your poison like a virus
But I can't get enough
Of this Sweet Intoxication

Point of No Return

This burning sensation
Of flames ready to consume me
This fever taking over my brain
The intense heat on my skin
The heat of your gaze as you watch me from across the room
If you love me
Let me go
I must escape
Don't keep me chained in this cage any longer
Stuck in the inferno of your burning desire
You want me
You need me
You captured me
I fear you
I hate you
I try to run away
Don't bring me to your point of no return
You're thirsty
Thirsty for my love
You want to drink it in
You're hungry
Hungry for my affections
You want to taste it
But I will never give it to you
Never
Never
Never

Saying Sorry

Why is it so hard to say,
A simple phrase said day by day
We hurt so many
With only us to blame
Yet when the time comes
Consumed by fear
And on the run
Running away from responsibility and shame
Just why is it
So impossible to leave our lips
Two words that make it
Slightly better
Than all the stinging pain
It seems so easy to say
But then I realize
It's pride that's in our way
In my moment of weakness
This is what I say
I'm sorry you hate me
I'm sorry you think it's fair
I'm sorry I'm moody
I'm sorry I actually care
I'm sorry for every little thing
You seem to blame me for
I'm sorry that
You've closed your door
I'm sorry we both feel the pain
Of the grudge increasing day by day
I'm sorry life
Is at it's hard point
But what kills me most is saying
I'm sorry that you can't accept me
And then you force me away
I'm sorry is just
All I can say

Crying

I'm tired of you
Sick of it all
This overwhelming feeling
My mind trapped in walls
Aching chest
Throbbing mind
Choking in
This invisible bind
Sitting amongst
Broken glass
That made up my heart
Empty lies
That tore me apart
My whole life I thought I was weak
But really I was strong
Though now I'm tired of this useless strength
I want to be weak for once
I want to stop crying
And hold it in
I want my emotions to stop flowing
I want to stop feeling sorry
I want to stop my unfeeling
But I don't want to be dead
I'm going to lose my strength
And suck it up
Cause crying in front of others
Is the greatest sign of strength
But I am now
No longer proud
I'm tired of all the tears I've shed
I want this senselessness to end
To finally be numb
In shameful bliss
I am now waiting
for my crying and strength to cease

Pretend

Sometimes it's fun to pretend to be normal
When everyone knows you're strange
Sometimes you like the feeling of running
Even if running through the rain
Pretending the droplets are rainbows and sunshine
When everyone can't see the pain
Sometimes you want to pretend
To be this great happy person
Sometimes it's nice to pretend
That the mirror of you isn't broken
That old friends were still there
That ties weren't severed
Love wasn't lost
People hated you never
It's easy to pretend
To avoid questions of
"Are you okay?"
Even though things
Might never be "okay"
When everything around you is changing
When everything you know is a lie
The special person in your heart is gone from your sight
It's so much easier to lie and say
"I'm fine"
Even when the other person can see right through your lies
They won't say a word
They'll just give you some space
So throw on a happy face
And saunter around
That fake smile you're wearing
Is the best form of pretend

Mirror Mirror

Mirror Mirror on the wall
I see why you are so false
Only showing what others see
Never showing who is really me
Copying others
Never yourself
While showing lies
You have a hidden truth
Within the depth of our reflections
We see our pasts, futures, and now
Fake dimension
Trapped in the glass
I see nothing
But everything joins me
Desire eriseD
False eslaF
True eurT
Me eM
You uoY
Let's play a game oh Magic Mirror
Can you guess my name?
That's right of course
So you know me
But can you guess your own?
Nope that's mine!
You're not me
Because you're just a reflection
So a rock is what you get
For being fake
And deceiving all around
Crash
Crack
Shatter
Mirror Mirror on the wall
You're finally broken
Once and for all

Breaking the Expectations

I looked in the mirror
And saw a girl
Who seemed perfect in every way
She was made of what everyone wanted of me
Docile and respectful
Seriously smiling
Wanting to please
But who that is
Is not me
Her smile was fake
Her eyes were dull
How she looked at me
Unnerved me to the bone
Staring at the mirror
With her staring at me
I screamed and screamed
With her copying me
She mocked me with their expectations
My fury was escaping
My want to be free
I broke the mirror
With my terrified screams
Still staring in the mirror
My reflection changed
With me still screaming in it's face
But suddenly I started to laugh
Beneath the cracks and broken glass
Beneath the lies and broken expectations
There stood who I was
Laughing with me
With bright eyes and a scowling face
Crazy and strange
Playful and sweet
Only wanting to please myself
I broke the image of me
Everyone expected
Now I'm free with myself
Now I can be me
No more staring in the mirror
Where I broke the expectations

In the Mirror

In my mirror was another world
A world long lost
With secrets untold
Secrets long lost
Secrets filled with horrors to behold
Creatures unseen
Distorted reflections
He was haunting me
She was stalking me
They would deeply intrigue me
But now
I'm scared to say the least
But a long time ago
The girl pulled me in to visit
And tormented me endlessly
Her brother was away
And with me was only her
Evil hidden by a pretty face
Thin white hair framed her heart shaped face
Large serpent eyes bore into mine
Bat wings carried me far and high
Long claw like nails caressed my face
She hit me
She kicked me
She stabbed me and whipped
A tortured soul and her fear
I feared her
And she feared me
But one day
I was overcome
I took the knife
And up it swung
Through her heart
The blade was plunged
I ran far away
To the mirror in the forest
Her brother was chasing after me
Through the mirror I went
And back home I was
His hand was out of its glass barrier
I took the mirror in my hold
And crashed it down
The mirror on the floor
Was gone in pieces

I killed the boy
In the mirror
Before he came to life

Rose Petal Tears

A Darkness so Vast
a Hurt so Cruel
Tears of Petal Roses
clear liquid
turning to drops of crimson
then becoming velvety pieces once on the ground
staining the blank sheets down and down
She's imprisoned
Held Captive
No One Knows Why
A void she's in
in A void she sleeps
in A void she asks
On the blank sheet she cries
A cry for no apparent reason
Tears for herself
Tears for the void
Tears for the darkness
Tears of why
Tears of Petal Roses
in the void she hides
in the void she cries
in the void she dies
And The Petal Roses Fade Away

Too Late To Turn Away

You gave them hope
Left them desire
You teach them lessons
On life long fire
But slowly
One by one
Your treacherous deeds cannot be undone
Formulated a plan
That went greatly astray
Sweeping up the ashes
And pieces of yesterday
Slowly but surely
They were betrayed by you
Slowly but surely
You felt the freeze too
The freeze that caused
A burning sensation
In the depths of your heart
A fiery anticipation
You watch them slowly
Fall to their death
Wasting only
Your useless breath
You watched their eyes turn
From love to hate
You screamed out their names
But did not fight fate
You could have stopped it
You could have tried
You could have saved them
They needed not to die
The path you walk
Is filled with horrid deeds
The path you walk
Greatly misleads
Now forever more
On this path you stay
For it is far too late
To turn away

Waves of a New Day

I have waited so long
We sing a sad song
I stand in the rain
It washes away my pain
No one sees my tears
So I hide all my fears
Things have to change
Nothing is in my range
You can change it all
Or just let me fall
Please take away the sorrow
Others will surely follow
Everyone wants some peace
Just give us that in the least
We wait, wait, and wait
Someone needs to set us straight
What will you say?
I stand here waiting, for the waves of a new day

www.ingramcontent.com/pod-product-compliance
Ingram Content Group UK Ltd.
Pitfield, Milton Keynes, MK11 3LW, UK
UKHW051136260726
13967UKWH00010B/3074

9 781105 786495